Dear SanTa Claws

Letters to Santa from Cats

Dear SanTa Claws

Letters to Santa from Cats

Compiled by E.J. Sullivan

SWEETWATER
PRESS

SWEETWATER
PRESS

Dear Santa Claws: Letters to Santa from Cats

Copyright © 2007 by Cliff Road Books, Inc.
Produced by arrangement with Sweetwater Press

ISBN-13: 978-1-58173-716-5
ISBN-10: 1-58173-716-5

Book design by Miles G. Parsons
Illustrated by Neal Cross

Dear Santa Claws,

    Cat food is smelly and dos not taste gud. Why do I have to eat it? Plees bring me something gud too eat.

                  Your frend,
                  Tigger

Dear Santa Claws,

I em verry sory that I shredded that toilet papper. I promis I just acidently bumped it and then it startd rolling and things got out of hand. I no I wus a badd kittie but I won't do it again so please bring me some of thet can food with the little foil lid.

Yur frend,
Harry

Dear Santa Claws,

I don't feel so good. These hairballs are the worst. If you could get my people to take me to the doctor that would be good.

Many thanks,
Lulu

Dear Santa,

The cat across the street is staring at me. Every day she sits in the window looking straight over here at me in my window. I think she likes me. Please help me let her know how I feel.

Faithfully,
Marvin

Dear Santa,

It is cold out here. When I look in the windows everybody looks warm. There is plenty of room for more kitties to go inside where it is warm. Can you please bring me a warm home too?

Thank you,
Sally

Deer Santa Claws,

I wuld verry much like a collar with a tag on it that jingles. Like the one that my friend Fluff has. But please make my collar pink. That way my people will know where I am when I get lost.

Sincerely,
Miss Priss

Dear Santa,

We reely need some steps around here that will help us get up on the counter easier.

Best wishes,
Cleo and Leo

Dear Santa Claws,

Do they have cats at the North Pole?
If they do I wuld like a job working for
you. I em verry gud at testing toys to see
iff they wil break. I wuld be gud at that
job. If you have room for me I will be
waiting for yu.

Sinseerly,
Mittens

Dear Santa Claws,

Do you have kitties at the North Pole? Cause I wud like to come and be one of your cats. I cud live in your barn and catch the mice, as that is what I do already here. Please?

With fond regards,
Catwick

Dear Santa Claws,

I would like a goldfish of my very own. I promise all I would do is watch it swim around.

Your friend,
Fats

Dear Santa,

I see how my people buy and sell things on the Internet. I would like to sell our dog. Can you help me?

Your friend,
Kit Kat

Dear Santa,

   I can't help noticing that my people always take the dog on vacation but leave me at home. While I enjoy my private time having the run of the house, I don't see why I can't go on vacation some time and let the dog stay home. If you could arrange this I would be forever grateful.

Cheers,
Cecil

Dear Santa Claws,

My friend Kissy says you are not real, and that only stupid little kittens believe in you. I am not stupid and I believe. I want some canned food for Christmas, and am planning on leaving some milk out for you. Don't bring anything for Kissy.

Sincerely,
Henrietta

Dear Santa,

 Please bring me a boy or girl of my own for Christmas. I am lonely here in this cage, even if it is crowded with all kinds of other kittens.

Thanks,
Muffin

Dear Santa,

I no I don't look like much but I clean up gud. I wud make sumone a gud cat. Cud you please send me a owner? Thank you verry much.

Your frend,
Clyde

Dear Santa Claws,

 Is there such a thing as a dog alarm? If so, we want one.

Suzy and Lucy

Dear Santa,

    I em not shure how to spell this but I wuld like for Christmas a dog ketcher.

              Sinceerly yurs,

              Barney

Dear Santa,

If you could bring a brand new fresh and expensive piece of furniture for me to scratch on I will be your friend forever.

Fondly,
Tina

Dear Santa Claws,

The cat next door says they have a garbage can that opens when you jump on a pedal. This sounds too good to be true but if there is such a thing, please bring us one. We are in the white house with the blue shutters at the end of the road.

Thank you,
George

Dear Santa,

In this house the childrun go too summer kamp. Ken you please make there be a summer kamp for dogs too? I need a brake!

Blackie

Dear Santa Claws,

We would like more than anything if you could bring us a bird. It would be so fun to chase, and we promise we would not hurt it, only play with it.

Thank you! We are leaving you some tuna fish tonight.

Toby and Moby

Dear Santa,

    Could you please bring us a lock for the cat door as the dog from next door keeps coming in here and we are sick and tired of his ugly mug. Plus he eats all our food!

                      Thank you,
                      Miff and Buff

Dear Santa,

Do not worry about myself but if you could just find homes for my kittens I would be grateful.

Thank you.
Martha

Dear Santa Claws,

    If you have some sleeping pills we would very much like this to put in the dog food. Bring a lot.

Bix and Trixie

Dear Santa Claws,

Please I would like whatever you recommend for repairing scratches and gouges in woodwork. This would keep me out of a whole lot of trouble. Also some large fish.

I will be your friend forever,
Luther

Dear Santa,

I would like a set of earplugs as the barking of this Shih Tzu is driving me bonkers.

Mel

Dear Sannta,

My people are moving away. I herd them talking about this and they are putting everythin in boxes. They tuk me to the vet and ask the vet ken he keep me an find me a new home! They think I kan not understand whut they say but I heer every word, Santa. Pleese do not let them leev me and move away!!

Sinceerly, your frend
Kip

Deer Sanna Claws,

Is ther anny way you culd bring sum peece and quiet around heer? I like too take naps and need several every day (at leest 5 or 6) and they brout home this new babie that crys all the tyme – there is no way I ken sleep! Pleese help.

Luna

Dear Santa,

  We have two birds, also two dogs, some guinea pigs, turtles, and two horses. Why do I have to be the only cat? Could you please bring me a friend.

Your pal,
Luther

Dear Santa,

I am not sure when Christmas comes but I am awfully hungry right now. Could you bring me some cat food? You will find me near the dumpster in the parking lot.

Yours truly,
Mookie

Dear Santa,

Something smells rely bad in the garbage and I would like to have it very much. Thank you fer your help.

Bootsie

Dear Sannta Claws,

I am a verry special cat and I would like to have some more mirrors around heer so I can admire myself more. If you could bring the kind that go up from the floor that way I would not have to keep jumping upp on things to see myself.

Love,
Felicity

Dear Santa,

There is a new cleaning lady coming here who has gotten rid of the dead bugs and dustballs and old socks, so things are not so much fun around here now. Could you bring us some nasty stuff like that to play with?

Thank you,
Honeycat and Gipper

Dear Santa,

I em pretty sure there is a dog next door who would like to eat me but I cant see so good. Would you bring me a pair of glasses so I can see him coming and not get et?

Thanks a lot.
Fred

Dear Sannta,

Please bring me some mouse-scented perfume, I think that wuld drive my Tyrone crazy!

Luv,
Katie

Dear Santa Claws,
    I wuld like:
A toy that squeaks
Milk (regaler, not skim)
A new coller (red or blue, NOT pink!)
                Thank you!
                Charlie

Santa Claws,

I wuld like more than anything else for my boy to come back home. He got big and packed up some stuff and books and things and went away and I miss him verry much.

Sadly,
Ginger

Dear Santa Claws,

That was me who left you the mouse with the glass of milk. I hope you liked it and that you will put some catnip in my stocking this year.

Your friend,
Trey

Dear Santa,

Those kats in the house next door keep coming in our yard and pretending that it is their yard. It is NOT their yard, it is MY yard. There are 3 of them tho and only 1 of me and I am kind of little. Ken you bring us a BIG fence?

Sassy

Dear Sandy Claws,

If you see us when we are sleeping, I am sorry about what I did the other night. I did not mean to pull the curtain down, only to look at something important up at the top. Please bring my mother a new curtain and everything will be okay.

Thank you,
Pickles

Dear Santa Claws,

    I just hav to know – iz your sleigh pulled by dogs? That iz what our dog says but I don't believe him. I hope it iz not pulled by dogs as it wil be verry unpleasant around heer when you arrive.

                      Hoping sincerely,
                      Peanut

Deer Santa,

I reely like sootcases. I like to gett in them. My owners get madd when I doo that but I like them more than anything. Culd you bring me a sootcase for my own? It kud be just a small 1.

Thankk U!

Sporty

Dear Santa,

I only have one eye and that is okay. I am not complaining. But I was thinking that an eyepatch would make me look a little more attractive with the ladies, if you know what I mean. They tend to be a little skittish around me and see, I'm getting on up in years but an old boy still likes to step out now and then. An eye patch would make this old guy a lot more presentable.

Your faithful friend,
Toby the Cat

Dear Santa,

Do you only bring presents to good cats? I heard from Snickers next door that was how it worked with boys and girls. I have been mostly good, except that time I got on the dinner table and ate the leftovers. I don't know how that happened, I honestly don't. One minute I was on the floor and the next I was gnawing turkey. It was a nightmare. I hope you can overlook this.

Many thanks,
Willow

Dear Santa Claws,

When you come down the chimnee look careful in there, becuz I left you a present that I caught myself for you outside. I caught it a few dayz ago so I hope it is still ok.

Sinceerly,
Rocket Man

Deer Santa Claws,

Do you know the Eester Bunny and the Tooth Fairy? If so cud you pass this letter on to them too? I want a ball with a bell in it for xmas butt I also likes eggs verry much and my tooth came out when I was chewing on the chair an I need to no whut to doo with it.

Thank you.
Savannah

Dear Santa

All I would like is a dog containment unit.

Thanks,
Vera

Dear Santa,

If I have to ride in the car to go to the vet why can't I have a kitty sick bag? This is getting most embarrassing and undignified. Thank you.

Yours truly,
Caesar

Dear Santa,

I hope you hav a merry krissmas and if yoo hav a kittie it is verry lucky.

Cisco